HANDBELL METHOD

...CTAVES

BY BEVERLY SIMPSON

T0068883

Material revised and expanded from *Ringing Basics* by Beverly Simpson (Shawnee Press).

Back cover photo courtesy of Malmark, Inc., Plumsteadville, PA
Handbells and accessories courtesy of Layton Avenue Baptist Church, Greenfield, WI
Handchimes courtesy of St. John's Lutheran Church, Brookfield, WI

ISBN 978-1-4584-3669-6

Visit Hal Leonard Online at
www.halleonard.com

Contact Us:
Hal Leonard
7777 West Bluemound Road
Milwaukee, WI 53213
Email: info@halleonard.com

In Europe contact:
Hal Leonard Europe Limited
Distribution Centre, Newmarket Road
Bury St Edmunds, Suffolk, IP33 3YB
Email: info@halleonardeurope.com

In Australia contact:
Hal Leonard Australia Pty. Ltd.
4 Lentara Court
Cheltenham, Victoria, 3192 Australia
Email: info@halleonard.com.au

PREFACE

The **Hal Leonard Handbell Method** is a step-by-step approach to the art of handbell ringing. The basics of music and bell ringing are presented and reinforced through explanations, exercises and pieces. The pieces are designed for learning and practice, but they may also be used for performance.

It is assumed that:
- Little, if anything, is known about ringing handbells or handchimes.
- Little, if anything, is known about reading music.
- You want to learn to ring bells and/or chimes musically without damaging them (or yourself!)
- You consider the art of bell ringing worthy of respect.
- You expect to learn how to read music.
- If you already know how to read music, you realize that there are special techniques to learn and practice for bell ringing that go beyond music reading.
- If you are a professional musician who has all kinds of degrees and plays all kinds of instruments, you realize that this is another instrument to be learned. There is much to learn about the art of handbell ringing! This book will provide you with basic, fundamental information upon which you may develop your own style, be creative and find joy.

In a handbell choir, **every ringer is important**—no one is more important than another. Beautiful music is made when ringers work together as a team and are tuned in to each other. Interdependence is the key to success!

NOTE TO DIRECTORS

Exercises and pieces are designed to teach one concept at a time and to provide practice. They are deliberately short and varied. Success should come quickly as choir members discover the fun of ringing bells. Music readers will move quickly through the pages as they learn the special knack of ringing. Non-music readers will move more slowly. This may be a major learning experience for them, so be prepared to allow whatever time is needed. The goal is for everyone to reach a similar level of competence and confidence. There should be little need for marking music or for other such "crutches." This method will provide a solid foundation for years of competent, musical and enjoyable ringing.

The Appendix in the back of this book includes stretches, warm-ups and a helpful Director's Guide for many of the pieces. These tools will help you make the most out of your rehearsal time and ensure that everyone has fun—including you!

CONTENTS

RINGING BASICS

About Handbells 4

About Handchimes 5

Setting Up & Distributing the Bells 6

How to Ring & Damp a Handbell 7

Legato Ringing 8

MUSIC BASICS

The Beat of Life 9

Keep Pace with Your Eyes 10

Music: A Language of Symbols 11

The Grand Staff 12

Naming the Lines & Spaces 13

READING & RINGING

Bell Assignments on the Staff 14

Reading & Ringing from the Staff 15

    Opus I (whole notes) 16

    Opus II (ties) 18

    Opus III (half notes) 20

    Opus IV (quarter notes) 22

    Opus IV Variation (L.V.) 24

    Opus V (dotted half notes) 26

    Ring Joy 28

Accidentals, Key Signatures & Time Signatures 30

PRACTICE & PERFORMANCE PIECES

Checklist 31

    Little Brown Jug 31

    Lightly Row 32

    Morning Song 33

Time for a Rest or Two 34

    Crazy 34

Staccato Techniques 35

    A Little Jazz for Bells 36

Dynamics & Tempo 38

    Hymn of Thanks (tower swing) 39

    Silesian Melody 42

    Brother John's Canon (shake) 45

Dividing the Beat (eighth notes) 48

    A Little Quicky (sight-reading) 49

Dotted Quarter Notes 50

    The Combo 51

    America 52

Pick-Up Notes 54

    A Folk Tune 55

    O Come, Little Children 56

APPENDIX

Stretches & Physical Warm-Ups 58

Rhythm Warm-Ups 60

    Ring a Scale with Chords 61

Director's Guide 62

ABOUT HANDBELLS

The handbell is a sturdy but breakable instrument. The casting is made of bronze alloy and has no protective coating. Therefore, **avoid touching the metal to your skin**. Wear gloves to prevent fingerprints, and always wipe down the bells with a polishing cloth after each rehearsal. A sneeze, laughing fit or explosive talking can spray invisible drops of saliva on a whole octave of bells! You may see mysterious spots on the castings later, which are probably caused by saliva. These marks won't affect the sound, but over time they will diminish the pristine look of your bells.

The manufacturer's guarantee on your bells will not cover misuse or accidents. **Safeguard the casting**. Do not:
- drop a bell on the floor or any hard surface.
- clang two bells together.

Make sure the bells are dry and polished when you put them away. Store the bells in their cases in a dry room, and avoid getting moisture inside the cases. If the bells have been used outside in cold temperatures, let them warm up before storing to avoid condensation.

Polish the bells after each rehearsal with a polishing cloth. Once or twice a year, use a cream polish especially formulated for handbells (other kinds may be too abrasive). When you polish, either with cream or a polishing cloth, rest the bell on its lip on a paper-covered table. Use an up-and-down motion to polish around the casting. Do not hold the bell in mid-air, as this exerts too much pressure on the handle and handguard.

Tuning is affected by changes in temperature. Your bells have been tuned in carefully-controlled temperature and humidity conditions. If you just brought them inside from a cold temperature, let them warm up before using them.

The **strike point** is the place on the casting determined by the manufacturer to be the best-sounding spot for the clapper to strike. This is indicated by a small vertical line etched inside the casting near the lip. The side with the strike point is the front of the bell. The side opposite the strike point is the back of the bell.

Never set the **springs** too tight. They should be just tight enough to prevent the bell from ringing when you don't want it to, and loose enough so that it will ring with a gentle wrist motion. Set the back spring tighter than the front spring to minimize the chance of an unwanted back-ring.

American-made handbells have a bell logo on the handle to indicate the backside (opposite the strike point). Always set the bells on the table with the logo on top to ensure that you pick up the bells correctly (see photo below).

Foam padding cushions the bells and prevents chipping the lip on a hard table surface. Padding also keeps the bells from rolling around. The resonance of plucking, martellato and mallet strikes is determined by the thickness and texture of the padding. Purchase 3-inch or 4-inch padding from a bell company or supplier. (Upholsterer's padding may or may not work, and you probably won't save any money.) Drape a large velvet or corduroy cloth over the padding.

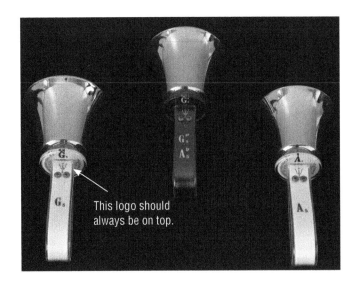

This logo should always be on top.

ABOUT HANDCHIMES

The handchime (or Choirchime®) is a sturdy instrument made of aluminum, with the clapper on the outside. It resembles an oversized tuning fork. Naturals are silver, while sharps and flats are black. Each tube is clearly labeled with its pitch, and also shows where the note is located on the staff.

Handchimes cost significantly less than handbells, and are ideal for use with children, the elderly and the disabled. They are lightweight, easy to handle, and will not be damaged if dropped by accident. You do not need accessories such as gloves or foam padding, although you should use a cloth cover on the table. When used together with handbells, handchimes provide extra interest and tonal color. They are especially effective when used for a melody line. Handchimes can be cleaned by simply rubbing them with a soft cloth (dry or damp).

In this book, the term "bell" will refer to both the handbell and the handchime. Most of the same music can be used by either instrument.

How to Ring and Damp a Handchime

1. Hold the tube near the bottom with the clapper facing you. The tube should be held upright, tilted back a little so the clapper head is open at the farthest possible distance from the strike point. This is the "ready to ring" position.

2. To ring, thrust the chime forward so the clapper strikes, or taps, the tube. Then bring the chime back to the "ready to ring" position immediately.

3. To damp (stop) the sound, simply touch the tines (prongs) to your body. Here are several appropriate damping motions.

   a. Turn your wrist inward so the tines touch your chest.
   b. Tilt the chime back so the tines touch your chest.
   c. Bring your elbow back so the tines touch your side.
   d. If only one chime is being used, you may damp on the opposite side of your chest.
      (This is only for those who will never use two chimes—perhaps because of a disability.)

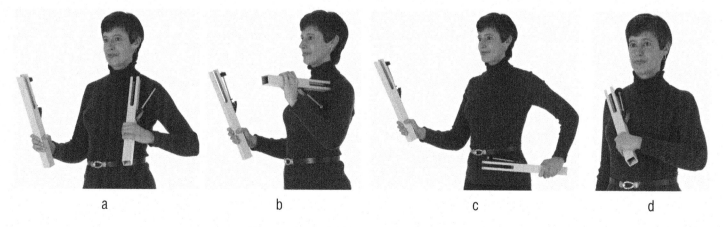

a   b   c   d

Choirchime is a registered trademark for handheld chime instruments produced by Malmark, Inc., Plumsteadville, PA.

SETTING UP & DISTRIBUTING THE BELLS

A complete set of handbells is **chromatic**, meaning there is a bell for each half step in pitch. Each bell is numbered by **octave**. The lowest octave in a three-octave set begins with C4. All the bells in that octave are labeled "4" up to B4. The next octave begins with C5 and goes up to B5, followed by C6 to B6. The highest bell is C7.

For three octaves of bells, you will need at least 21 feet of table space (24 is better). Standing behind the tables, start with C4 on the left end and lay the bells out in note order from left to right. Place each sharp (#) bell to the right of its natural, and more forward on the table (like the black keys on a piano).

The 37 bells should be distributed to ten people (or positions), as shown below. Bells in parentheses are shared by two ringers.

Position 1	C4	C#4	D4	(D#4)		**Position 6**	F5	F#5	G5	(G#5)	
Position 2	(E♭4)	E4	F4	(F#4)		**Position 7**	(A♭5)	A5	A#5	B5	
Position 3	(G♭4)	G4	G#4	A4	(A#4)	**Position 8**	C6	C#6	D6	(D#6)	
Position 4	(B♭4)	B4	C5	(C#5)		**Position 9**	(E♭6)	E6	F6	(F#6)	
Position 5	(D♭5)	D5	D#5	E5		**Position 10**	(G♭6)	G6	G#6	A6	A#6/B♭6

Notice that B6 and C7 do not appear in this list—they are "unassigned bells" which may be given to any position able to ring extra bells. (The director may need to ring these at first.)

THE IDEAL BELL SET-UP

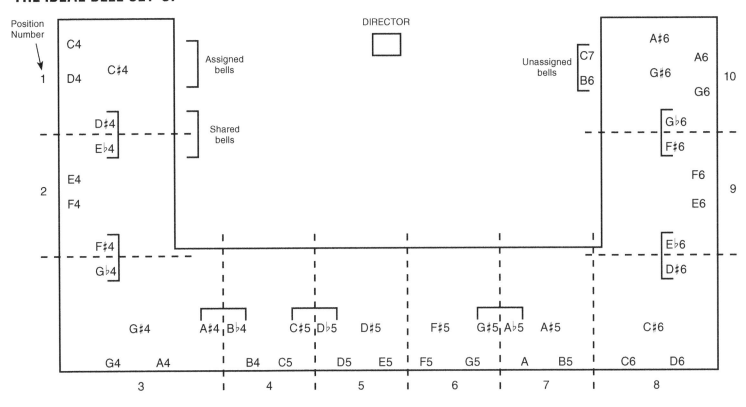

A "U" shape allows everyone to hear each other well. Try to practice this way even if space does not permit the "U" shape for performance.

Start with two positions per music stand. This creates partners who can help each other, especially with page turns. Also, the cost of music is cut in half and the beautiful bells can be better seen by your audience. Members with vision issues, however, may need their own stand.

Notice the "shared bells" in the diagram above. Some bells have two names, depending on how that pitch is notated in the music. C# is the same as D♭, for example, so the C person will ring C# and the D person will ring D♭.

HOW TO RING & DAMP A HANDBELL

First Things First!

- Wear clothing that covers your shoulders and chest—for the safety of the bells and your skin!
- Don't wear pins, jewelry, zippers or name tags that could make contact with the bell casting.
- Always wear cloth gloves when handling the bells.

The Grip

- English handbells ring to the front and back. Make sure the bell logo on the handle is facing you before picking it up.
- Hold the bell upright, with the handguard resting on your thumb and index finger. Your fingers go **around** the strap, not through it. Your knuckles should face to the side.
- Grasp the handle firmly (but not a "death grip").

How to Ring

- Ready-to-Ring Position: Rest the bell against your chest/shoulder, tilted so the clapper drops back toward you.
- Without ringing, use a circular arm motion to slowly move the bell down your body, out, up, and back to your shoulder. (Think of a Ferris wheel.) Watch the clapper and keep it back as you make the circle.
- Repeat this silent motion several times before continuing to the next step.
- As you pass the bottom of the circle (at approximately eight o'clock), flick the bell forward to ring it. Watch the clapper as it strikes the casting and then drops back to the ready-to-ring position.
- Practice ringing with one hand, then the other hand, and finally alternating hands.
- Use wrist action to ring the smallest bells. As the bells get larger, use more arm, shoulder and back muscles.

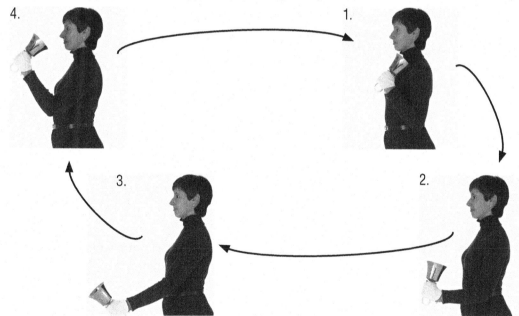

How to Damp (Stop the Sound)

- Simply touch the bell casting to your chest just below your shoulder.
- The entire casting will be vibrating, so the entire side of the casting should touch your body to stop all the sound.

NOTE: Sometimes you will need to damp a bell on the table in order to pick up a new bell. Lay it down gently, but firmly, to stop all the sound. (You don't need to damp on your shoulder first.)

Volume Control

The strength and speed at which the clapper strikes the casting determines the volume. A strong, fast thrust will be loud; a slower, more gentle motion will be soft. Practice for control from very soft to very loud.

LEGATO RINGING

Legato (pronounced "leh-GAH-toe") means smooth and connected. For handbells, legato ringing means to damp one bell at the exact same time the other bell rings. There should be neither gaps nor overlaps in the sound from one bell to the other. Think of it like walking: as one foot goes down, the other lifts. As one bell rings, the other damps.

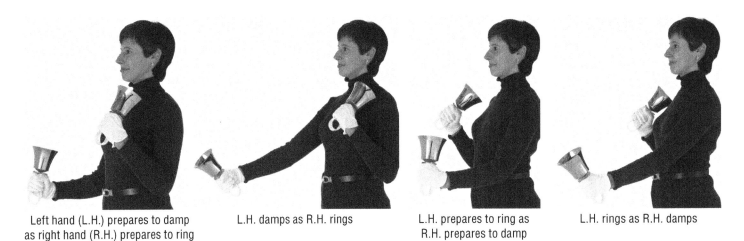

Left hand (L.H.) prepares to damp as right hand (R.H.) prepares to ring | L.H. damps as R.H. rings | L.H. prepares to ring as R.H. prepares to damp | L.H. rings as R.H. damps

Be patient with yourself as you learn to coordinate these motions—it takes practice!

Ring a Scale

A **scale** is a series of adjacent notes played in order. Starting with Position 1, ring all the natural bells sequentially from left to right (C Major scale). The director should ring B6 and C7 at the top. Then ring the same scale back down from right to left.

- Follow the director's count to maintain a steady rate of speed.
- Each bell should be damped at exactly the same time as the next bell rings. (Once again, think of walking.)
- Try to match the volume and speed of your neighbor.

Ring a Chord

A **chord** is a group of notes that are played together. Ring all the C, E and G bells together to make a C Major chord. Let the sound continue as you count to four. Ring the chord together several times, following the director's count.

- All bells should ring at exactly the same time.
- You don't need to damp between repeated chords—just keep the circular motion going and damp after the final chord. Everyone should damp at exactly the same time.

NOTE: If your group members can already read music, see page 61 for more practice with legato scale/chord ringing.

Ring an Arpeggio

An **arpeggio** (pronounced "ar-PEH-jee-oh") is a chord broken up into individual notes. Using the same C, E and G bells, start with C4 and ring one bell at a time. Go up and then back down without damping—all bells should continue sounding until the end.

Start rehearsals with a warm-up. Ring: left-right-left-right. Check the stroke and damping. Ring as if your bells are on springs—they bounce up and back after striking. For stretches and rhythm warm-ups, see pages 58-60.

THE BEAT OF LIFE

Every living creature has a beat. Feel your pulse—are you a living creature? If there is no beat, there is no life. It is the same with music. For it to be "alive," there must be a beat. This concept is so crucial to bell ringing that you will learn about the beat and rhythm basics first.

Look at a clock with a second hand. The second hand is moving steadily around the face of the clock, marking time as it passes. Time is always marching on, whether you are aware of it or not!

With everyone looking at the same clock, watch the second hand and count 16 seconds aloud together.

To read music, as with printed words, your eyes move from left to right in a straight line. Your eyes must move ahead at a steady beat, like the passing seconds. Instead of circling the clock, your eyes move forward.

Next, count out 16 seconds aloud in groups of four. Focus your eyes on each number below as you count.

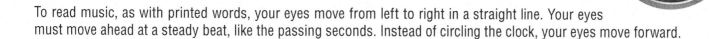

Now we'll replace each comma with a vertical line, and use two lines at the end instead of a period.

1   2   3   4 | 1   2   3   4 | 1   2   3   4 | 1   2   3   4   ‖

Time is "measured out" in music. In the example above, we are measuring out 16 seconds in groups of four.

The vertical lines are called **bar lines**, and the space between two bar lines is called a **measure**.

| ← measure → | ← measure → | ← measure → | ← measure → ‖

Double bar lines are used at the end of a piece or section.

KEEP PACE WITH YOUR EYES

Bell ringing involves many things to coordinate—eyes, ears, arms, wrists and hands! For the following exercise, pick up any two adjacent bells, with the lower-pitched bell in your left hand.

- The director will count four preparatory beats to set the **tempo** (rate of speed). Everyone should count these beats aloud with the director.

- Count all beats aloud together as you ring your bells according to the instructions below. (Measure numbers are marked above the bar lines.)

- Keep your eyes focused on the numbered beats, moving in time with the beat.

Measure 1: Ring L.H. bell and let it ring through beat 4.

Measure 2: Ring R.H. bell and let it ring through beat 4.

Measure 3: Ring L.H. bell again.

Measure 4: Ring R.H. bell again.

Count: 1   2   3   4

1   2   3   4 | 1 → 2 → 3 → 4 — | 1 → 2 → 3 → 4 → | 1 → 2 → 3 → 4 → | 1 → 2 → 3 → 4 → ‖

                                left   right   left   right

> Remember to damp your L.H. bell as your R.H. bell rings, and vice versa.

More About Eye Movement

Read the following "poem" silently to yourself:

We love music, we love the bell.
We'll count together or go to... pieces!

Now read it aloud together. Notice that:

- Everyone had to read at the same pace in order to stay together.

- Eyes moved naturally from word to word as you read.

- Eyes moved at the same tempo as you read.

The same concept applies to reading music. Your eyes move steadily through each measure, focusing on one beat at a time.

MUSIC: A LANGUAGE OF SYMBOLS

A **symbol** is a sign used in place of words. In music, **notes** are symbols that indicate time values.

This is the symbol for a whole note: **O**

- A whole note equals four beats. (Keep thinking of beats as seconds in time for now.)
- It is placed in the "beat 1" slot within the measure.
- It is rung on beat 1 and the sound continues to the end of beat 4.

In the following exercise, ring left-right-left-right as before. Focus on the line of notes and move forward as indicated by the arrows, in time with the counting. Measure numbers are shown above the bar lines.

Count: 1 2 3 4 | **O** → 2 → 3 → 4 → | **O** → 2 → 3 → 4 → | **O** → 2 → 3 → 4 → | **O** → 2 → 3 → 4 → ‖

       1   2   3   4

      left   right   left   right

Damp the bell that is resonating as you ring the other bell. Keep each bell moving in a circular motion as it resonates.

Be aware of where each beat is located within a measure. In the following measures, on which beat would each "X" fall, judging by its placement?

A. __ __ __ <u>X</u> ‖ B. <u>X</u> __ __ __ ‖ C. __ __ <u>X</u> __ ‖ D. __ <u>X</u> __ __ ‖

As you progress through the book, you will learn to read the following note symbols. The sound must continue for the full duration of each note value.

O	Whole note = 4 beats
♩ (half)	Half note = 2 beats
♩	Quarter note = 1 beat
♩.	Dotted half note = 3 beats
♪	Eighth note = ½ beat
♩.	Dotted quarter note = 1 ½ beats

THE GRAND STAFF

A **staff** is a set of lines and spaces on which music is notated. How would you like to read music from this staff? We need at least eleven lines and spaces for bell music, but this would be ridiculous!

11 ————————————————————————————
10 ————————————————————————————
9 ————————————————————————————
8 ————————————————————————————
7 ————————————————————————————
6 ————————————————————————————
5 ————————————————————————————
4 ————————————————————————————
3 ————————————————————————————
2 ————————————————————————————
1 ————————————————————————————

Separate the eleven lines into two groups of five lines and four spaces, called the **grand staff**. The middle line (line 6) is placed on "standby." Such lines are called **ledger lines**—they temporarily extend the staff when needed. Ledger lines may appear either above or below a staff. In bell music, it has been agreed that the C5 ledger line will always appear above the bottom staff.

————————————————————————————
————————————————————————————
————————————————————————————
————————————————————————————
————————————————————————————
- -
————————————————————————————
————————————————————————————
————————————————————————————
————————————————————————————

The staff lines alone, however, don't tell us enough. We need **clef signs**. There are several different clefs, but only two are used in bell music. The lower staff uses a **bass clef**, and the upper staff uses a **treble clef**. Letter names are determined by the clef.

Treble Clef

Brace

Bass Clef

Treble Staff

Bass Staff

NAMING THE LINES & SPACES

Music notes sit on a line or in a space. Lines and spaces are named using the letters A through G. A note has the letter name of the line or space on which it is located.

The bottom line of the bass staff is G (think of G as in "Ground Floor"). The next space up is A. Go up in alphabetical order with a letter name for each line and space. When you reach G, start over again with A. Include the space B above the bass staff and a ledger line for the C above it (often called "Middle C").

In bell music, Middle C is the highest note marked on the bass staff. The next D is found in the space below the treble staff. Once you reach the top space of the treble staff (G), ledger lines are used again for A, B and C.

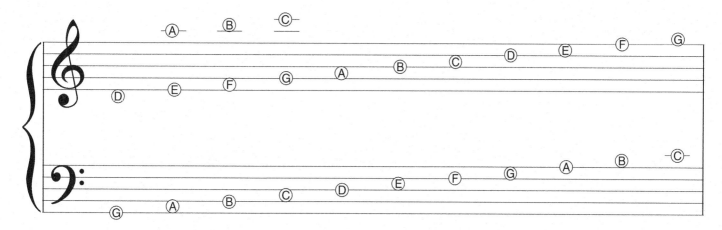

Numbered Bells & Placement on the Staff

Did you notice that each letter name was used more than once in the grand staff above? To distinguish between letter names, there is a number beside each letter on the bell handles. The number tells you in which octave that bell belongs. All bells in a particular octave share the same number (see below). Numbers change on C.

A Three-Octave Set of Bells on the Grand Staff

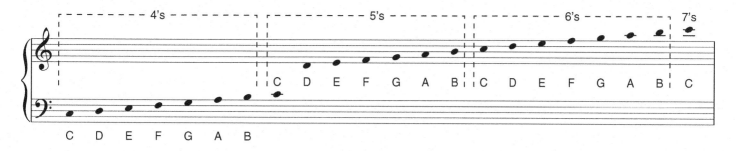

C4 and C7 are the lowest and highest bells, respectively, in a three-octave set.

You don't need to learn the entire staff all at once! You will be assigned only one line and one space, with their corresponding bells. Stay with one position for a period of time to get familiar with reading the notes, but don't be afraid to change positions later. When you change, however, move several positions away to avoid confusion.

BELL ASSIGNMENTS ON THE STAFF

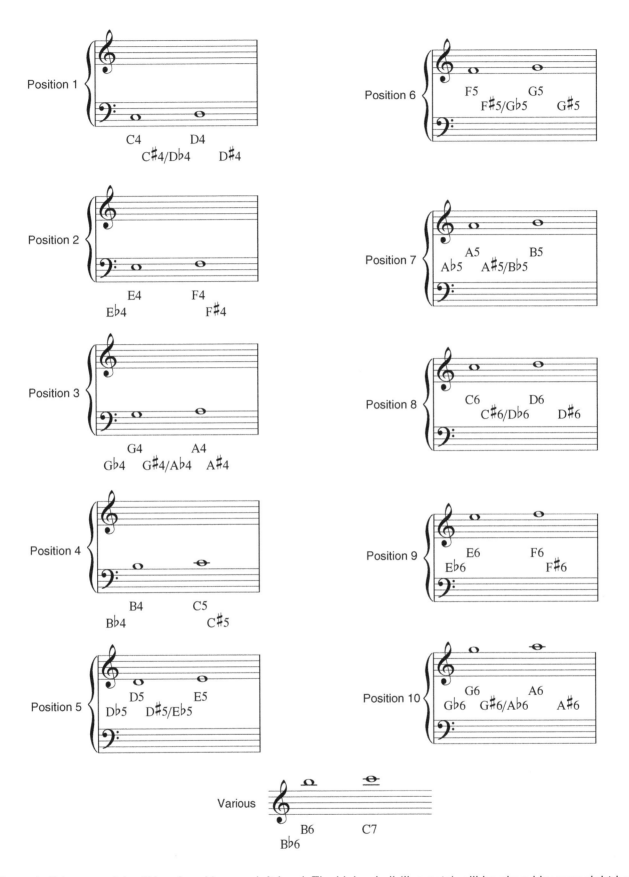

The lower bell (space note) will be played by your left hand. The higher bell (line note) will be played by your right hand. Each position also includes the sharps and flats of each note. Refer back to page 6 for an explanation of shared sharp/flat bells.

B6 and C7 should be assigned to the ringers best able to handle them in a given piece. An 11th person (possibly the director) may ring them in the early stages, but it is important for ringers to learn to ring extra bells as soon as possible. B6 and C7 are assigned to various positions throughout this book.

READING & RINGING FROM THE STAFF

1. Locate your assigned space and line on the staff.

2. Count four beats in each measure.

3. Keep pace with your eyes through each measure.

4. Ring when a note appears on your line or space. The only way to know when to ring is to count!

5. Position 9 rings B6, Position 10 rings C7 (see instructions below).

EVERYONE COUNTS IN A BELL CHOIR!

NOTE: In this book, beat numbers appear between the **staves** (plural of "staff"), while measure numbers (abbreviated with "M") appear above the treble staff.

Example A

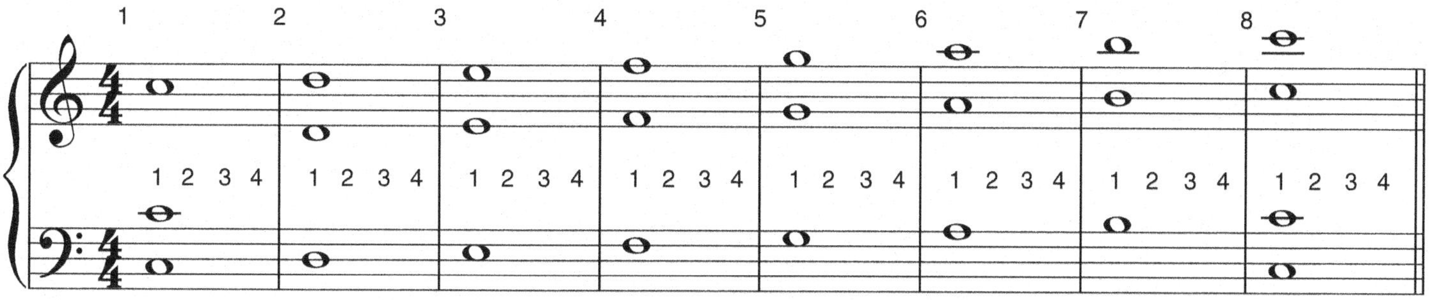

Position 9: Table damp F6 on beat 1 of M.5, pick up B6 and ring it on beat 1 of M.7.
Position 10: Table damp A6 on beat 1 of M.7, pick up C7 and ring it on beat 1 of M.8.

Example B

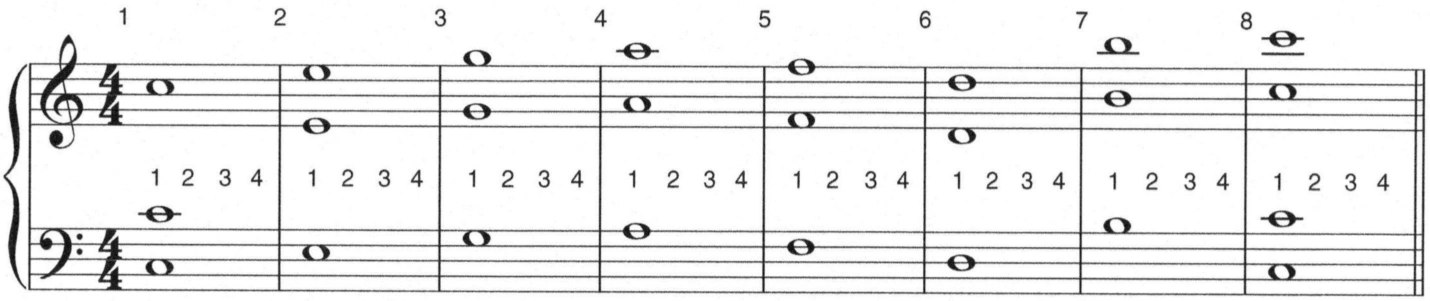

Position 9: Table damp F6 on beat 1 of M.6, pick up B6 and ring it on beat 1 of M.7.
Position 10: Table damp A6 on beat 1 of M.5, pick up C7 and ring it on beat 1 of M.8.

Plan your actions and keep your bells in order! Mark your music to remind yourself when to change bells, if necessary.

PREPARING TO RING "OPUS I"

In this book, space notes are always left-hand bells. Line notes are always right-hand bells. This will not be true when you advance into more complex music, but it is helpful in the beginning stages. (Aren't you glad you only have two hands?)

"Bells Used" Chart

A small staff at the beginning of a piece shows which bells are needed. Position numbers may be indicated here as well. It's not part of the music—it's just for reference.

Steps to Ringing

1. Locate your assigned space and line on the staff, and focus your eyes on that spot.

2. Count one measure first to set the tempo. Everyone should count out loud together.

3. Ring when a note appears on your line or space.

4. All notes in "Opus I" are whole notes. Each chord will sound on beat 1 and continue through beat 4. Damp on beat 1 of the next measure, unless your note is repeated.

Helpful Hints

- Notice where your notes appear in the music, and which hand will play them.
- When the piece begins, focus on your line and space as you count each beat.
- Keep counting, even if you have nothing to ring for several measures.
- Play all space notes with your left hand. Play all line notes with your right hand.
- Do not damp between repeated notes.

Offset Notes

M.8 and M.10: A4 and A5 are offset from B4 and B5 on the staff so they can be clearly seen. However, they are still rung on beat 1 with the rest of the chord. Notice that G5 is also offset in M.11. Offset notes are very common in music notation.

OPUS I

By Beverly Simpson

Bells used: 20

Position: 1   2   3   4   5   6   7   8   9   10

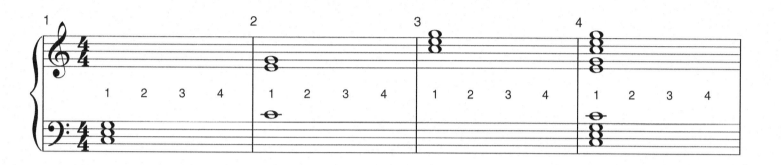

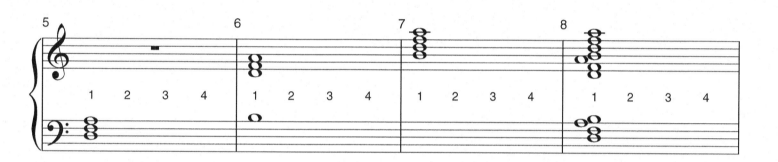

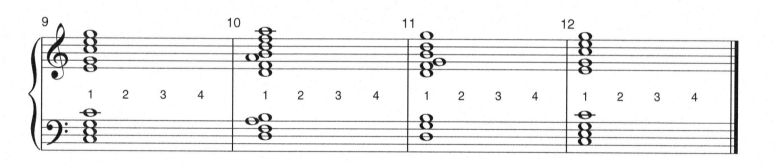

PREPARING TO RING "OPUS II"

Review "Steps to Ringing" and "Helpful Hints" on page 16.

To Damp or Not to Damp—That Is the Question

- Damp if your note is NOT in the next chord.
- DO NOT DAMP if your note is repeated in the next chord.

Examples:

M.2, beat 1: Damp all bells played in M.1 (none of these bells are in M.2).

M.3, beat 1: Damp all bells played in M.2 (none of these bells are in M.3).

M.6, beat 1: Damp C4 only. All other bells are repeated from M.5 (ring the new note G6).

M.10, beat 1: Damp C4 and C7. All other bells are repeated from M.9 (except G6 again).

Attention, Position 9!

Use your right hand for both F6 and C7. Here's how it works:

M.8, beat 1: Table damp F6, pick up C7.

M.9, beat 1: Ring C7.

M.10, beat 1: Table damp C7, pick up F6.

M.11-12, beat 1: Ring F6.

M.13, beat 1: Table damp F6, pick up C7.

M.16, beat 1: Ring C7.

The Tie

This symbol ⌣ or ⌢ is called a **tie**. It connects notes of the same pitch. Do not ring the second note, but let the sound continue for the total time value of both notes. It is important to be precise!

M.15-16: All notes in M.15 are "tied" to the notes in M.16. These bells should continue to sound for a total of 8 beats.

M.16: Ring E5, G6 and C7 while the other bells continue to sound from M.15.

OPUS II

By Beverly Simpson

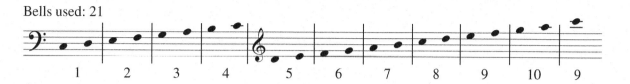

Bells used: 21

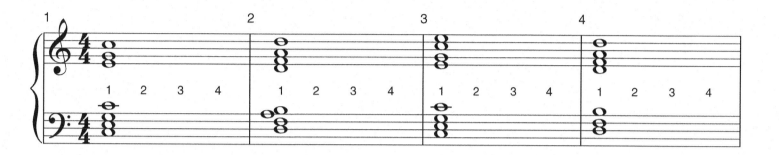

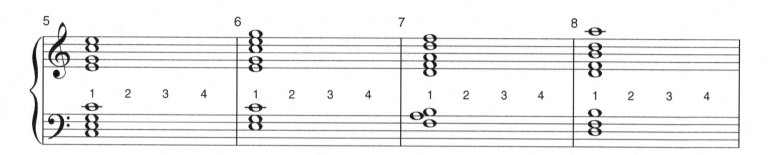

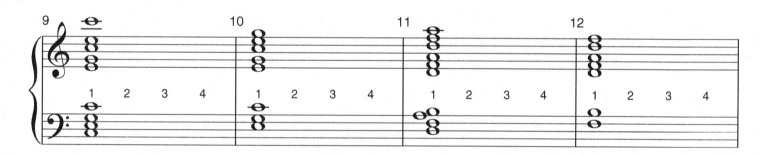

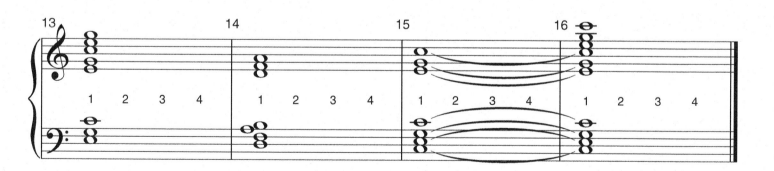

PREPARING TO RING "OPUS III"

Dividing the Whole Note (Half Notes)

If you divide something in half, you will have two equal parts. Dividing a whole note into two equal parts gives you two **half notes**. Objects consume space; music consumes time (beats). A half note consumes two seconds of time, or two beats.

4 beats = 2 beats + 2 beats

A half note looks similar to a whole note, but it is slightly smaller and has a stem. The stem can point either up or down, depending upon several things that you will learn about later.

A measure can have any number of beats. The first example below uses two-beat measures. The second example uses four-beat measures. The third example combines half notes and whole notes.

Count and clap these notes. Then, count and ring them.

Ex. A

| 1 | 2 | 1 (left) | 2 | 1 (right) | 2 | 1 (left) | 2 | 1 (right) | 2 |

Ex. B

| 1 | 2 | 3 | 4 | 1 (left) | 2 | 3 (right) | 4 | 1 (left) | 2 | 3 (right) | 4 |

Ex. C

| 1 | 2 | 3 | 4 | 1 (left) | 2 | 3 | 4 | 1 (left) | 2 | 3 (right) | 4 | 1 (left) | 2 | 3 (right) | 4 | 1 (left) | 2 | 3 | 4 |

Be alert to the cut-off beat for every bell. You should damp at the end of each note's duration. A half note on beat 1 should be damped on beat 3 (or re-struck if it's a repeated note).

Stopping the sound is just as important as making the sound!

Voice-Leading Lines

A diagonal line is used direct your attention to the movement of a melody line (or "voice") from one staff to another. In M.7-8 of "Opus III," the bass line moves from C5 in the bass staff to D5 in the treble staff. In M.9, the bass line moves from E5 in the treble staff to C5 in the bass staff. Voice-leading lines show that the notes going between staves belong with each other and should be connected.

OPUS III

By Beverly Simpson

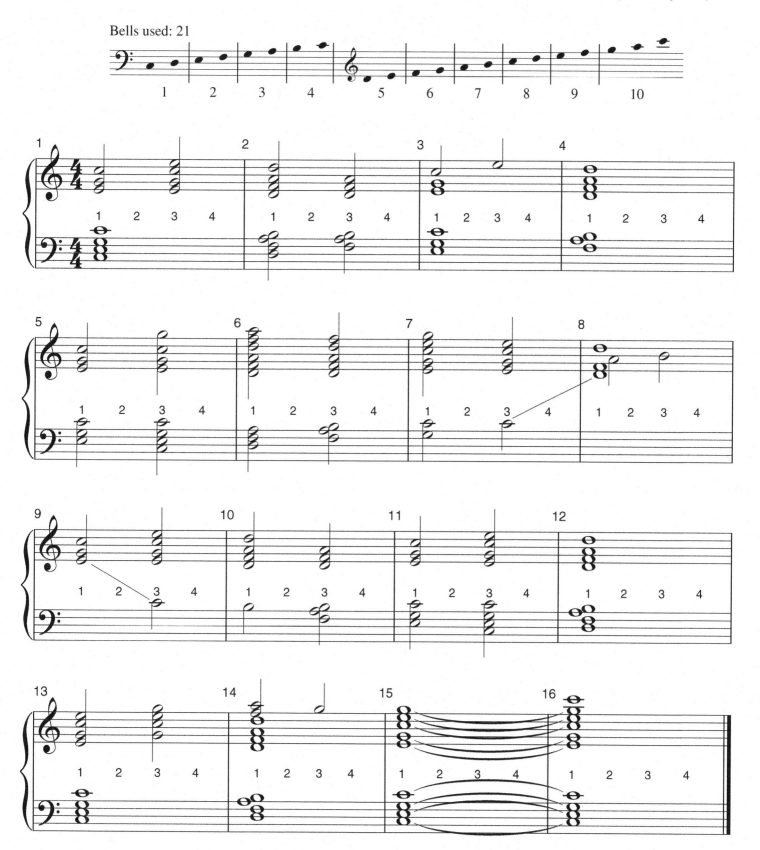

PREPARING TO RING "OPUS IV"

Dividing the Half in Half (Quarter Notes)

If you divide something into four equal parts, the parts are called "quarters." Likewise, dividing a half note in half gives you two **quarter notes**. A quarter note equals one beat.

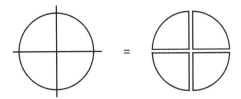

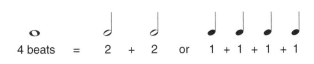

4 beats = 2 + 2 or 1 + 1 + 1 + 1

A quarter note looks similar to a half note, but it is solid black.

Look at the second hand of a clock. Clap several groups of four quarter notes at one-second intervals. Mark the first beat of each group by clapping louder on beat 1. This is called an **accent**, and it is indicated by: >
Accents may appear above or below a note.

In the following exercise, ring left-right-left-right. Accent beat one by ringing it louder. Don't forget to count!

Ex. A

1 2 3 4   1 2 3 4   1 2 3 4   1 2 3 4

For exercises B and C, ring with your left hand on downstem notes that sit below the line. Ring with your right hand on upstem notes that sit on the line.

Ex. B

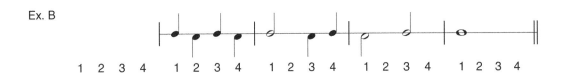

1 2 3 4   1 2 3 4   1 2 3 4   1 2 3 4   1 2 3 4

Ex. C

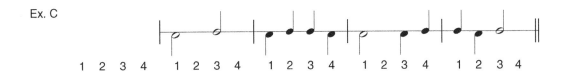

1 2 3 4   1 2 3 4   1 2 3 4   1 2 3 4   1 2 3 4

Repeat exercises B and C. This time:

> 1. Clap and then ring **only the upstem notes**. (Downstem notes = silence)
> 2. Clap and then ring **only the downstem notes**. (Upstem notes = silence)

EVERYONE COUNTS IN A BELL CHOIR!

OPUS IV

By Beverly Simpson

Did this piece sound familiar? The music in "Opus IV" is exactly the same as "Opus III," except all the note values are cut in half!

PREPARING TO RING "OPUS IV VARIATION"

Arpeggio

The melody and harmony are the same as "Opus IV," but instead of block chords in which all notes are played simultaneously, the chords are created one note at a time. A broken chord is called an **arpeggio**, as you learned on page 8.

Let Vibrate (L.V.)

When you see "L.V." in the music, **do not damp**. Let the sounds overlap each other, regardless of the note values. This creates a blended effect. Damp only when one of the following occurs:

- You see another L.V. which begins a new effect.
- You see a **damp sign** ⊕ which means to resume normal damping.
- You see the letter "R" which also means to resume normal damping.

In "Opus IV Variation," L.V. is placed below the bass staff when it applies only to the bass bells. It is placed between the staves when it applies to both staves (as in M.3). Here is a breakdown of how to damp this piece properly:

M.1: Bass bells L.V.

M.2, beat 1: Damp all bells sounding from M.1 and start a new L.V.

M.3: All bells L.V. in both staves.

M.4-8: Treble bells resume regular damping, bass bells follow L.V. signs.

M.9-12: All bells damp as usual.

M.13-14: Bass bells L.V.

M.15: L.V. from beat 3 to end.

Divide your group in half for the following exercise. Group A will clap the top line while Group B claps the bottom line.

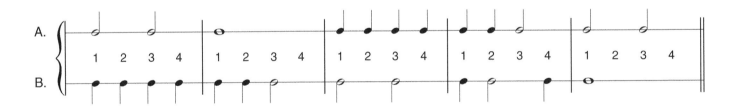

Switch groups and repeat the exercise. Then, try ringing bells for line A and clapping for line B, and vice versa. Have fun with it!

NOTE: "Opus III," "Opus IV" and "Opus IV Variation" can be strung together as a beginning performance piece. Proceed from one to the next without stopping.

OPUS IV VARIATION

By Beverly Simpson

PREPARING TO RING "OPUS V"

Dotted Half Notes

A **dotted half note** equals three beats. The dot placed after the note extends the note by half its time value. It is very important to understand this concept—think of it this way:

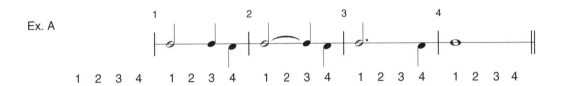

Ring exercise A below. (Upstem notes = right hand, downstem notes = left hand.) Notice that M.2 and M.3 sound the same, although they look different.

Ex. A

M.2: The half note is tied to the quarter note.
M.3: The dotted half note is shorthand for the tied notes.

A tie can (and does) connect notes over bar lines.

Ring exercises B and C below. When ties are connecting notes across bar lines, they cannot be shortened into dotted half notes.

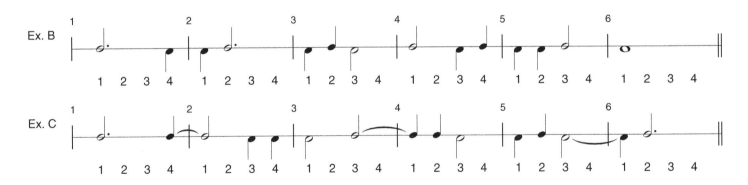

OPUS V

By Beverly Simpson

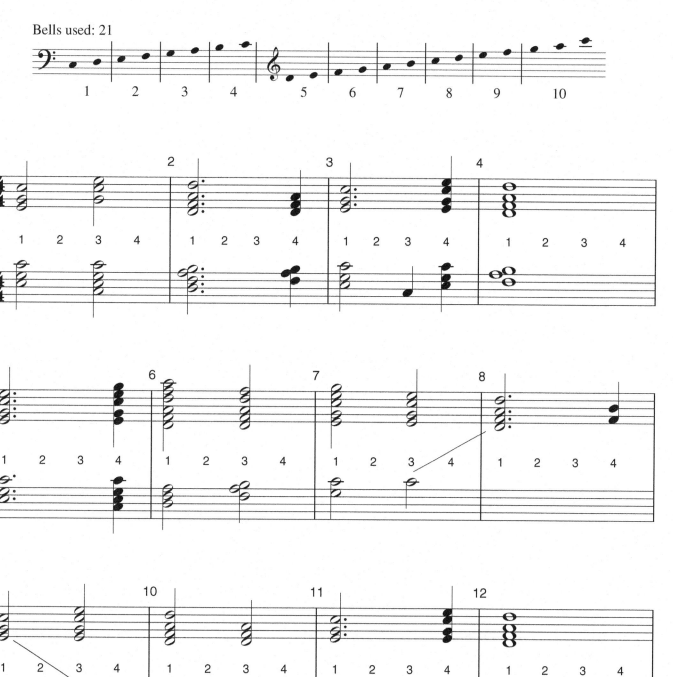

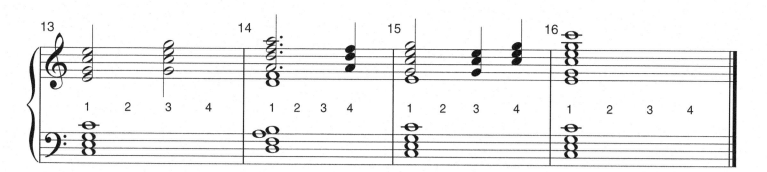

This piece can be rung successfully after only a few rehearsals.

This symbol ⌢ is called a **fermata**. It means to hold the note(s) longer than the strict time value. Always watch your director for the signal to either move on or damp (M.4, 20 and 28).

Position 7: Since B5 is not used in this piece, ring C7 with your right hand and A5 with your left hand.

RING JOY

By Beverly Simpson

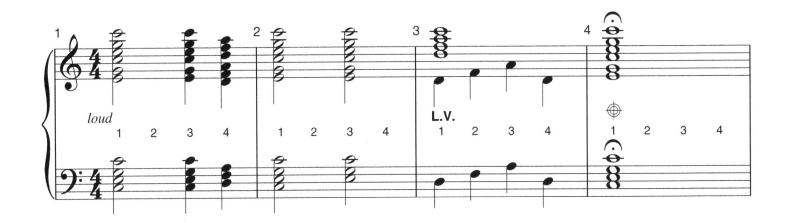

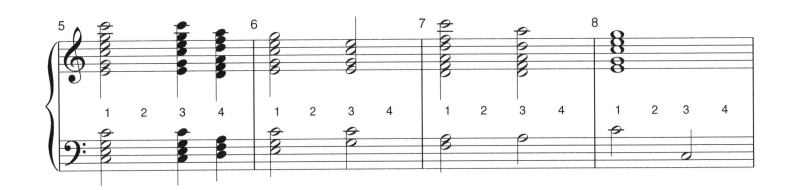

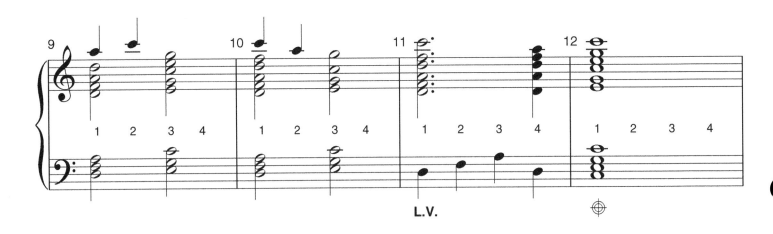

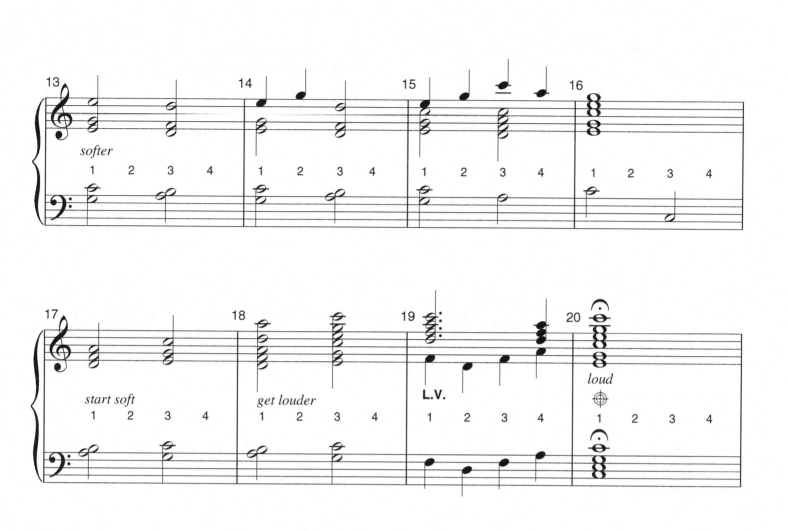

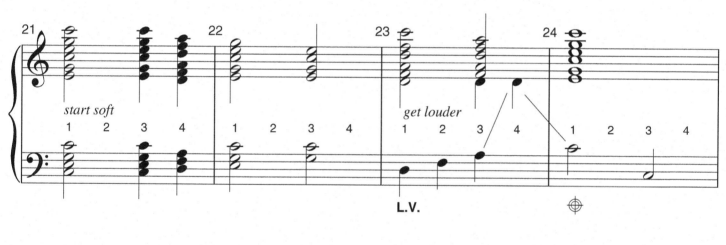

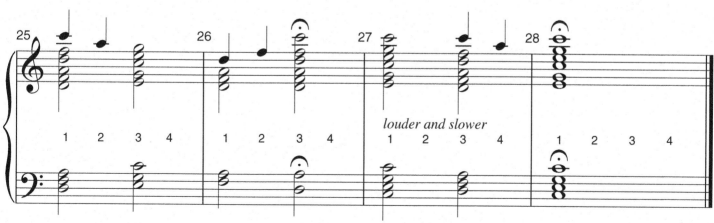

ACCIDENTALS, KEY SIGNATURES & TIME SIGNATURES

An **accidental** changes the pitch of a note. There are three main types of accidentals:

1. A **sharp** ♯ raises the pitch by one half step.

2. A **flat** ♭ lowers the pitch by one half step.

3. A **natural** ♮ cancels a sharp or flat, returning the pitch to normal.

The **key signature** comes after the clef sign in both staves, at the beginning of each line of music. The line(s) and space(s) on which sharps or flats appear in the key signature will be sharped or flatted throughout the entire piece.

You may have wondered what the stacked numbers at the beginning of your previous pieces mean. They are called the **time signature**. The top number tells you how many beats are in each measure, and the bottom note tells you which kind of note gets one beat. In this book, the quarter note will always get one beat, so the bottom number will always be 4.

Here are some examples of key signatures and time signatures:

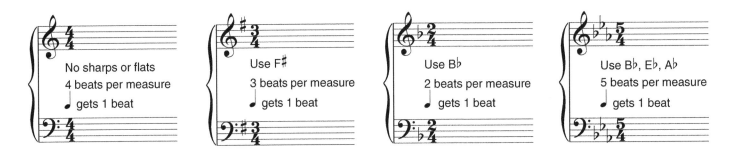

Regardless of the key signature, the pitch of any note may be altered within the piece by using an accidental. An accidental remains in effect only for the measure in which it appears; it is automatically canceled by the next bar line. (Sometimes a "courtesy" accidental is shown in the next measure as a reminder.)

EXCEPTION: If an altered note is tied over a bar line, the accidental remains in effect for the duration of the tied notes; then it is canceled. Notice how the notes are read in the following example:

Your bell assignment shows all the bells you will use in a particular piece. Place these bells in front of you; move any unused bells out of the way to avoid mistakes. Unlike other instruments, ringing in different keys is easy—as long as you start out with the correct bells!

CHECKLIST

FOR SIGHT-READING, PRACTICE & PERFORMANCE PIECES

1. **Bell Assignment** – Are all the bells you need in front of you? Are the extras out of the way?

2. **Key Signature** – Are there any sharps or flats shown after the clef sign?

3. **Time Signature** – How many beats per measure, and which kind of note gets one beat?

4. Look through the entire piece. Notice where you ring and if anything unusual happens. Look for accidentals, volume changes, or time/key signature changes.

5. When you begin the piece, count out loud (you don't have to shout). If you get lost, simply ask, "Which measure are we in?" When you find your place, re-enter on beat one of the next measure.

LITTLE BROWN JUG

By Joseph E. Winner
Arranged by Beverly Simpson

LIGHTLY ROW

Traditional
Arranged by Beverly Simpson

NOTE: Positions 4 and 5 have only one "regular" bell, so they are also assigned B♭6 and C7, respectively. Use your right hand to ring the high bell and your left hand for the easier half-note low bell. Mark your music and keep smiling!

MORNING SONG

Gaelic Melody
Arranged by Beverly Simpson

TIME FOR A REST OR TWO

(THERE HAS BEEN NO REST SO FAR...)

A note indicates sound, but a **rest** indicates silence. Each kind of note has a corresponding rest with the same time value.

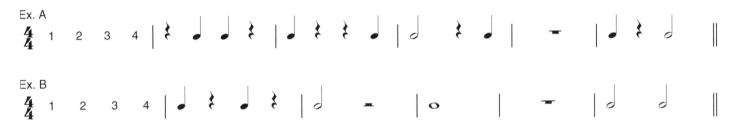

Quarter rest ♩ = quarter note ♩ in time value
Half rest — = half note ♩ in time value
Whole rest — = a whole measure of rest, regardless of the time signature

Occasionally, you will see dotted rests. Interpret their time value the same as dotted notes.

Clap the following exercises:

Ex. A

Ex. B

CRAZY

By Beverly Simpson

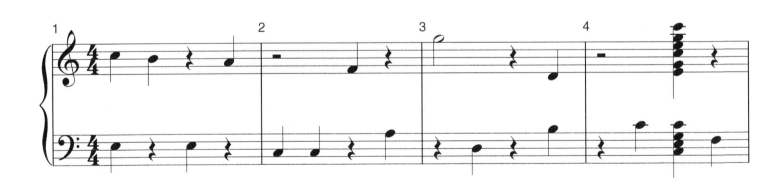

Bells used: 21

STACCATO TECHNIQUES

Staccato (pronounced "stuh-CAH-toe") means that notes should be detached. This is the opposite of legato. A note or chord to be rung staccato has a dot above or below it, like this:

The dot applies to all notes sharing a common stem. Staccato notes have a short, crisp sound—the opposite of legato. Legato is like smooth walking, while staccato is like hopping. There are several ways to achieve a staccato sound with bells:

1. **PLUCK** (indicated by **Pl.** and dots)
   Lay the bell on the table with the handle toward you. Hold the bell in place with one hand, lightly pressing it into the foam. Reach inside the bell with your other hand, grasping the clapper with your forefinger and/or thumb. Thrust the clapper against the casting. (E5 and lower: thrust downward. F5 and higher: thrust upward.)

2. **MARTELLATO** – or "mart" for short (indicated by ▼)
   Hold the bell horizontally above the foam padding, no higher than the diameter of the bell casting. The front of your fist should face downward with your knuckles to the side. Gently but firmly, thrust your fist down and strike the foam padding with the full body of the bell. The clapper will bounce off the casting to make a staccato sound.

3. **MARTELLATO LIFT** (indicated by ▼↑)
   After the martellato strike, immediately lift the bell to allow the sound to continue.

4. **THUMB DAMP** (indicated by **T.D.** and dots)
   Hold the bell as usual, except place your thumb on the outside of the casting. This produces a short, muted sound.

   NOTE: The addition of one or more fingers will be necessary for larger bells.

5. **MALLET** (indicated by ∔ or +)
   Mallets come in several varieties that are designed for specific bell ranges. Make sure you are using the correct mallet for your assigned bells. Strike the outside of the casting at the approximate spot where the clapper would strike the inside. The ∔ symbol means that the bell should be resting on the table when struck. The + symbol means that the bell should be held above the table when struck (usually not damped).

Any of the techniques on page 35 may be used to produce a staccato sound. If one is not specified in the music, use your own judgment and preference. Always be alert to the presence or absence of staccato dots.

PRACTICE: Ring a scale, chord and arpeggio, using a different staccato technique each time. Mix them up and have fun!

The following piece includes both staccato and legato ringing, so pay close attention!

Staccato and rung notes occurring on the same beat will have separate stems. (Notes with a common stem are treated alike.) In the treble staff of M.8, for example, D5 is staccato and G5 is rung.

Here's a breakdown of how to ring "A Little Jazz for Bells":

Position 1 rings B♭6, Position 2 rings C7. Mark your extra notes so you don't forget them.

  M.1-10: Pluck all bass staff notes, and also D5 in the treble staff.

  M.3-10: Half notes occurring on beat 2 are accented.

  M.11: Bass bells switch from plucking to ringing. Treble bells switch from ringing to thumb damping. **Attention, Position 8!** Ring C6 on beat 1, damp using your thumb on beat 3, and then play a thumb damp on beat 4.

  M.18: Treble bells switch back to ringing.

  M.19: Bass bells switch back to plucking.

  M.25-26: Let all bells vibrate. Treble bells should match the fading volume level of the bass chord.

Because of the staccato chords, the rung melody will stand out naturally. Even so, everyone should be aware of when they have the melody and play it with confidence!

A LITTLE JAZZ FOR BELLS

By Beverly Simpson

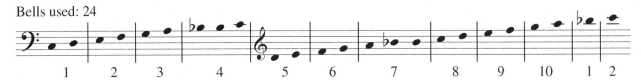

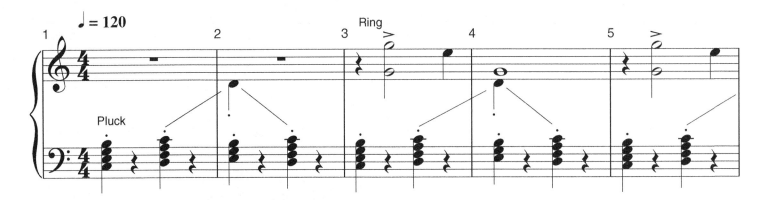

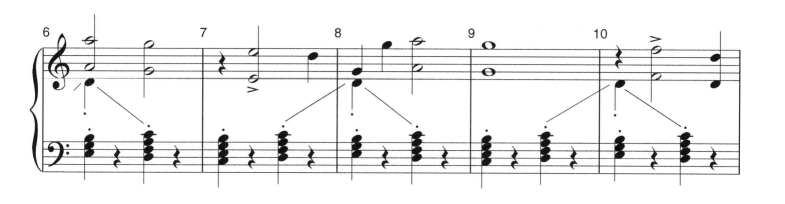

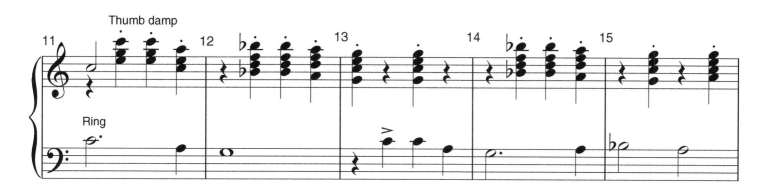

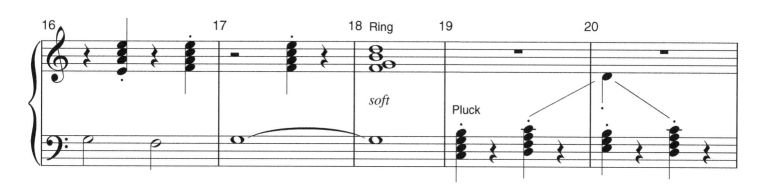

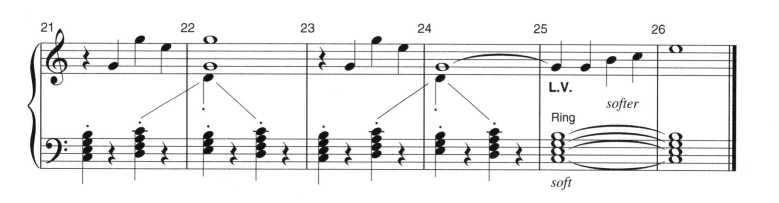

DYNAMICS & TEMPO

LEARN A LITTLE ITALIAN!

In physics, "dynamics" refer to energy—something that is active as opposed to something that is static. Music is active; it has energy. In addition to the obvious activity of music, there must also be emotional energy which is expressed by changes in volume and tempo. As you ring pieces, you will sometimes get louder or softer, speed up or slow down, etc. As your group becomes more skilled, even subtle changes will be noticeable.

By tradition, dynamic and tempo markings are Italian because music was first written, or notated, in Italy. These Italian terms are not difficult to learn, and they might come in handy if you should tour Italy someday!

Initial instructions for tempo and dynamics are printed at the beginning of a piece, and provide clues regarding the general "mood." Subsequent changes are marked in italics throughout the piece, and the Italian words are often abbreviated.

Common Symbols and Terms:

DYNAMICS (volume)

f	*forte*	loud
mf	*mezzo forte*	medium loud
mp	*mezzo piano*	medium soft
p	*piano*	soft
◁	*crescendo (cresc.)*	gradually louder
▷	*decrescendo (decresc.)*	gradually softer

TEMPO (rate of speed)

ritardando (ritard. or *rit.)*	slow down
poco rit.	slow down a little
molto rit.	slow down a lot
a tempo	resume the previous tempo (usually seen after a *rit.*)
allargando	broadly (louder and slower)
tenuto (ten.)	hold notes slightly longer than the time value for emphasis (less then a fermata)

Attention Position 8!

M.5, beat 3: Table damp D6, pick up C7 to ring in M.6 and M.7.

M.7, beat 2: Table damp C7, pick up D6 to ring in M.8.

Repeat this process throughout the piece and impress your audience! If it proves to be too difficult, your director can ring C7 instead.

HYMN OF THANKS
(with "We Plow the Fields and Scatter")

By Beverly Simpson
and Johann A.P. Schulz

WE PLOW THE FIELDS AND SCATTER (Refrain)

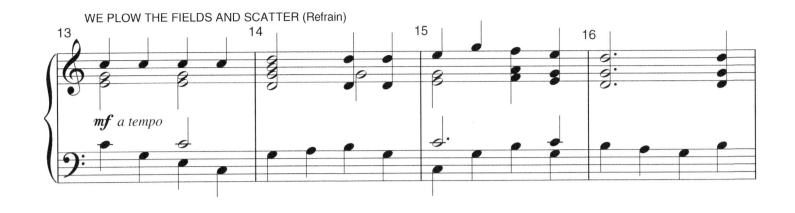

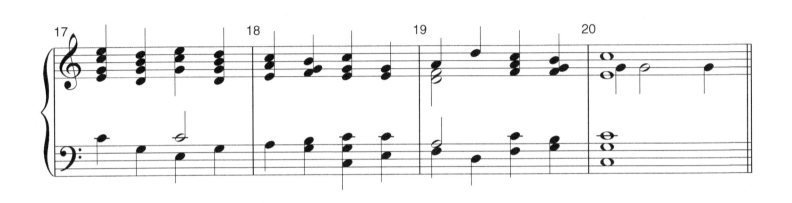

*New Technique: Tower Swing (TS or ↓ ↑)

After ringing a bell, swing your arm down and back. Then return the bell up to your shoulder. Perform these motions on the beats indicated by arrows in the music.

NOTE: You need space for this! If there's any danger of hitting something behind you, swing back no farther than your leg.

SILESIAN MELODY

Traditional
Arranged by Beverly Simpson

Bells used: 24

See page 63 for detailed ringing instructions.

Moderately

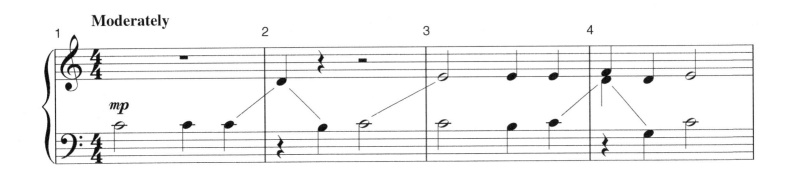

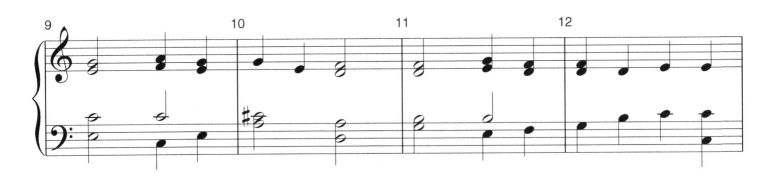

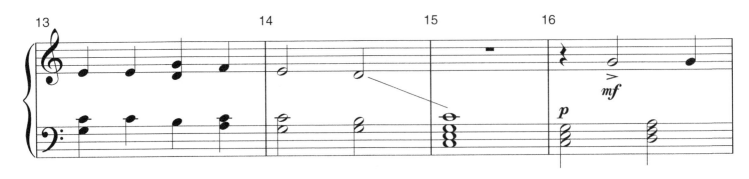

BROTHER JOHN'S CANON

Traditional French Melody
Arranged by Beverly Simpson

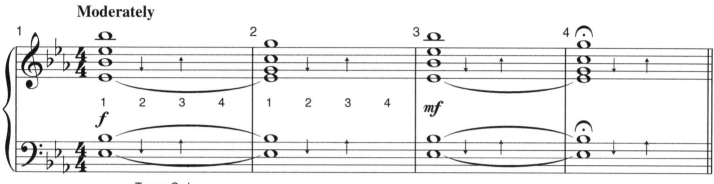

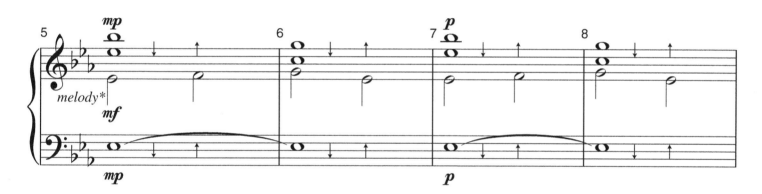

* This familiar tune is sometimes known as "Are You Sleeping?" or "Frère Jacques."

*New Technique: Shake (Sk. or ⌁)

Shake the bell rapidly back and forth so the clapper strikes both the front and back of the casting. (This is easier with smaller bells.) Wavy lines are often used to indicate the specific bells to shake. This technique makes it possible to *crescendo* on a sustained note. Shake for the duration of the note value.

DIVIDING THE BEAT

EIGHTH NOTES

We started with a whole note (4 beats) and divided it into two half notes (2 beats each). Then we divided it into four quarter notes (1 beat each).

Now we'll divide a quarter note into two **eighth notes**. An eighth note equals 1/2 beat. It looks like a quarter note with a flag on the stem. Pairs of eighth notes are usually connected by a straight beam. An eighth rest looks like this: ⅞

To count eighth notes, say "and" between the beats. Count and clap the following exercises (we'll use "&" instead of "and"):

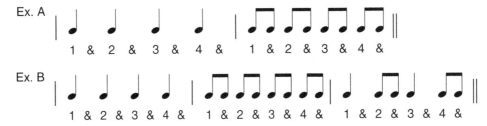

RINGING TIP

The longer the note value, the bigger the circle. The shorter the note value, the smaller the circle. When you are ringing eighth notes, keep the bells closer to your chest for quick damping. Maintain the circular motion, but smaller.

Count and ring this exercise. Keep a steady beat!
B6 and C7 may be assigned to any treble-staff position.

Look over the following piece for a few minutes, and then ring it through non-stop.
Ring at a careful tempo the first time, and then try it a little faster.
Repeat if you wish, then put it away. Bring it out another day!

A LITTLE QUICKY
(Sight-Reading Practice)

By Beverly Simpson

DOTTED QUARTER NOTES

A dot extends a note by half its time value. As you learned on page 26, a dotted half note is made like this:

A **dotted quarter note** is made the same way:

Count and clap the following exercises:

Ex. A

1 & 2 & 3 & 4 & | 1 & 2 & 3 & 4 & | 1 & 2 & 3 & 4 & | 1 & 2 & 3 & 4 &

Ex. B

1 & 2 & 3 & 4 | 1 & 2 & 3 & 4 & | 1 & 2 & 3 & 4 & | 1 & 2 & 3 & 4 &

Count and ring the following exercise.

- M.1-4 and M.5-8 will sound exactly the same, even though they look different.
- B6 and C7 may be assigned to any treble-staff position.

EVERYONE COUNTS IN A BELL CHOIR!

THE COMBO

By Beverly Simpson

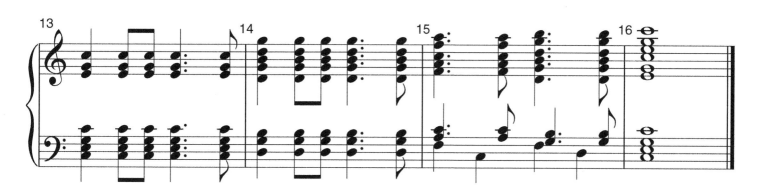

Count and ring the following exercises, using everyone's space and line note. Be ready to ring on any beat or half beat!

Downstem "space" notes = left hand
Upstem "line" notes = right hand

AMERICA

Words by Samuel Francis Smith
Music from *Thesaurus Musicus*
Arranged by Beverly Simpson

Bells used: 24

PICK-UP NOTES

Music does not always begin on beat 1. When a piece begins on a different beat, there is a partial measure that leads up to the first full measure. Notes in the partial measure are called **pick-up notes**. When a piece begins with pick-up notes, most phrases within the piece also begin with pick-up notes.

The first full measure will have a natural accent on beat 1. The pick-up notes lead up to beat 1 and are unstressed. The "missing" beats from the pick-up measure are often found in the final measure.

When counting preparatory beats, it is helpful to count one full measure **plus** the unused pick-up beats.

Clap the following exercises:

A FOLK TUNE

Traditional American Melody
Arranged by Beverly Simpson

O COME, LITTLE CHILDREN
(Christmas)

Words by C. von Schmidt
Music by Johann A.P. Schulz
Arranged by Beverly Simpson

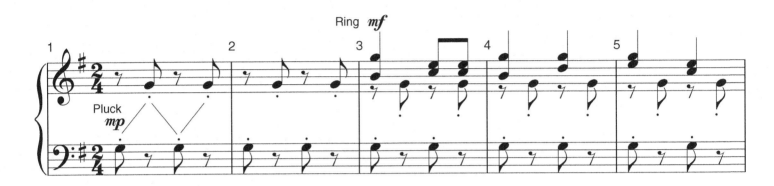

M.25-40 mallets: Strike with mallet while holding bell above table.
M.46 martellato: Strike casting horizontally into foam padding for a sharp, clean finish!

STRETCHES & PHYSICAL WARM-UPS

Athletes always warm up for their sport. Gymnasts are moving and stretching right up until it's their turn in the competition. Likewise, ringing bells is a physical activity and you need to prepare your body for action! Stretching for five minutes before each rehearsal will pay big dividends, preventing possible pain and injury.

Hold each stretch for at least five seconds. Breathe slowly and deeply.
Don't lock your knees; keep them relaxed and slightly bent.

1. Stand with feet slightly apart, arms at your side. Inhale and reach up, arms straight. Spread fingers, then clench fists. Exhale, inhale, exhale. Inhale and lower arms parallel to the floor. Exhale, inhale, exhale. Repeat.

2. With upper arms parallel to the floor, touch your shoulders with your fingertips. Shoulders back, press shoulder blades toward each other. Repeat.

3. Roll shoulders with a circular motion, front-up-back-down. Reverse direction and repeat.

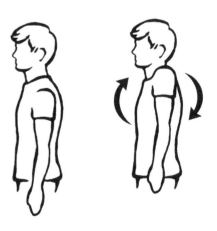

For a more extensive study of the physiology of bell ringing,
read *Healthy Ringing* by Susan Berry (Handbell Services, Inc.).

4. Move through the ringing circle (see page 7) with palms facing each other. Move down, out, up and back. Flick wrists at eight o'clock on the circle as if ringing; brush shoulders as if damping. Use one hand at a time, then hands together.

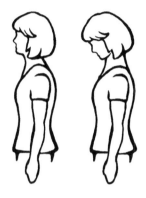

5. Stretch your neck by dropping and holding your head to your chest.

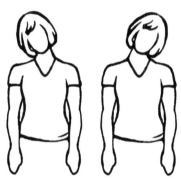

6. Drop right ear toward right shoulder and hold. Drop left ear toward left shoulder and hold.

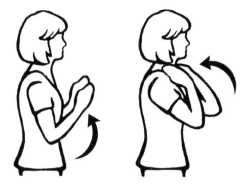

7. Bend at your waist slowly from side to side. S-t-r-e-t-c-h.

8. Give yourself a hug—you deserve it! While you're at it, give each other back rubs…

After ringing, cool down to relax the muscles that have been working hard. Repeat some of the above stretches. Loosen your wrists by rolling them in a circular motion. Move your arms up and down—fly a little!

RHYTHM WARM-UPS

1. Clap selected rhythms with note values that the group has learned.

2. Ring with left-hand bells on downstem (space) notes; right-hand bells on upstem (line) notes.

3. Ring left-hand bells only; right-hand bells = silence (rests)

4. Reverse step 3.

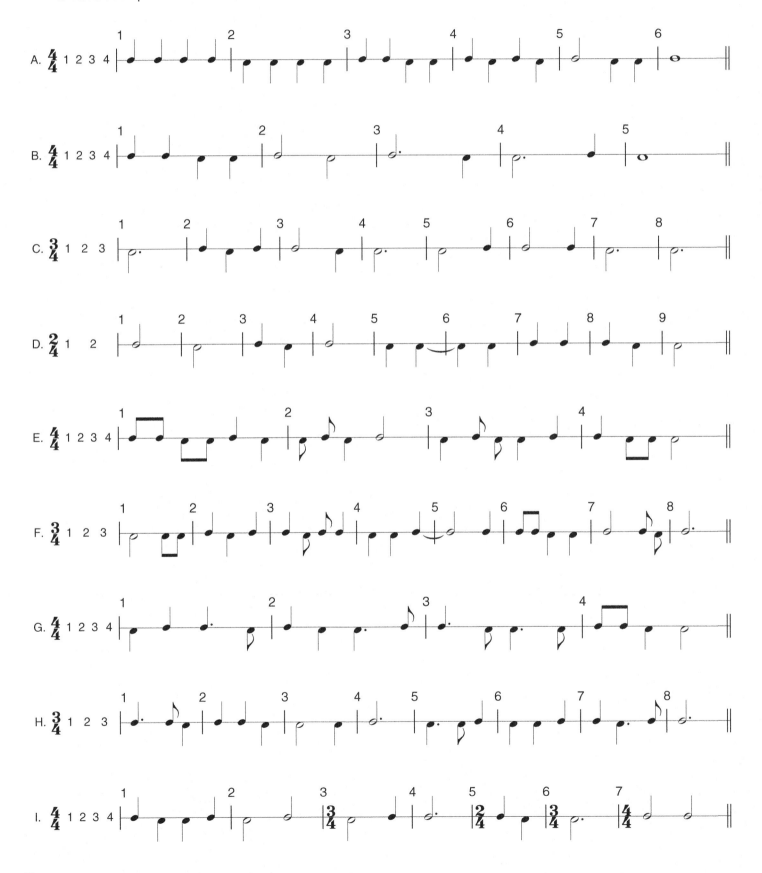

RING A SCALE WITH CHORDS

By Beverly Simpson

DIRECTOR'S GUIDE

This section provides helpful insights and rehearsal suggestions for several pieces in this book.

PREPARATION

Before ringing a piece, point out any potential problem spots, such as accidentals, tricky rhythms, key/time changes, etc. Encourage ringers to mark reminders in their music, but DON'T allow them to circle their notes (see FAQs on page 64). Beginning ringers sometimes want to label each of their notes by letter name or by which hand plays it. Not only is this habit hard to break, but it can also be confusing for others reading from the same page. Even worse, it eats up valuable rehearsal time! The goal is for everyone to learn to read **music**, not words.

EVALUATION

After ringing a piece, ask yourself (and the group) the following questions:

- Was the melody clear throughout, or did the chords sometimes drown it out?
- Did all the bells of each chord ring at the same time, or were there "ragged" spots?
- Were notes damped properly? If not, were they muddy or choppy (or a little of both)?

Ring the piece again, thinking about all of the above.

REHEARSAL SUGGESTIONS

Page 32 – Lightly Row
The melody in this piece is presented in octaves first. Once the chords begin in M.8, the octave melody should still be emphasized. It can be difficult for beginning ringers to be aware of who has the melody, but it is an important concept. Try this strategy:

- Ring the melody alone. Make sure the volume level is consistent from position to position.
- Ring the chords alone, a little softer than the melody. Again, check for consistency in volume.
- Put the parts back together and ring the whole piece.

Page 36 – A Little Jazz for Bells
Ring the melody alone from beginning to end. This will ensure that everyone knows when they have the melody.

- Treble bells have the melody from M.3-11.
- Bass bells take over the melody from M.11-18.
- Melody fragments appear again in the treble clef in M.21-26.

Page 39 – Hymn of Thanks
If your members started ringing in September and have covered the basics quickly, they may be ready to perform this piece in November for Thanksgiving. If not, it is appropriate for any time of year.

Frequently Asked Questions in "Hymn of Thanks"

Q: In M.5, how can I ring G5 on beat 4 when there's a half note on beat 3? Is that a mistake in the music?

A: *No, this type of "overlapping" notation is often used in bell music to distinguish between the melody and the harmony. After ringing the half note, ring again on beat 4 (a little stronger since it's part of the melody).*

Q: Why are some notes offset a little from the rest of the chord? Are they rung at the same time? (M.5, 7, 8, etc.)

A: *Yes, offset notes should be rung on the same beat as everything else. They are written slightly apart so the stem directions can be clearly seen, especially when they are part of the melody.*

Page 42 – Silesian Melody

M.1-15 (Stanza 1): Simple and steady. Legato melody should be louder.

M.16-20: This is a bridge between Stanzas 1 and 2. Upper notes should be louder. Accent beat 2 to emphasize syncopation and let chords be mellow.

M.29-36: This is a variation of the melody. Follow dynamic markings and be expressive.

M.34 (*tenuto*): Slightly extend the time value of each chord for emphasis.

M.37-40: This is a bridge between Stanzas 2 and 3. Upper notes should be louder than descending chords.

M.53 (*allargando*): Emphasize by getting louder and slower.

M.55 (tower swing): Ring on beat 1, swing down on beat 2, swing up on beat 3, hold on beat 4. Keep bells up until final damp.

The accidentals and extra bell in this piece require careful planning for Positions 1, 4 and 7. Go through the following steps with these ringers and encourage them to mark their music accordingly.
NOTE: Unless your Position 1 ringer is very experienced, you may need to ring C7 yourself.

No need for terror! Take it step by step and practice!

	Table damp	Pick up	Ring	Table damp	Pick up	Ring
Pos 1, M.33-34 (LH):	C4	C7	M.34, beat 1	beat 3	C4	M.36, beat 3
Pos 1, M.34, 38 (RH):	D4	C7	M.38, beat 1	beat 3	D4	M.42, beat 1
Pos 1, M.44-45 (RH):	D4	C7	M.45, beat 3	beat 4	D4	M.46, beat 3
Pos 1, M.49-50 (LH):	C4	C#4	M.50, beat 1	beat 2	C4	M.50, beat 4
Pos 4, M.48-51 (LH):	B4	C#5	M.50, beat 1	beat 3	B4	M.51, beat 1
Pos 7, M.49-51 (LH):	B5	C#6	M.50, beat 1	beat 3	B5	M.51, beat 1

Page 45 – Brother John's Canon

Sing this familiar song as a round with two or more parts. Then ring it at the same tempo.
Because C4 does not ring until M.54 and M.58, Position 1 is free to ring both B♭6 and C7.

M.45, beat 1: Table damp C7 and pick up C4.

M.54, beat 3: Ring C4 and B♭6 together.

M.57, beat 1: Table damp B♭6 and pick up C7 to ring in M.58 on beat 1. (Ring C4 on beat 3.)

There are **two** key changes in this piece, but they only affect Positions 5 and 8. Make sure these ringers understand when they need to change bells.

Position 5

M.35, beat 4: Table damp D5 and pick up D♭5 to ring in M.36 on beat 3.

M.44, beat 1: Table damp D♭5 and pick up D5 to ring on beat 3.

Position 8

M.31, beat 3: Table damp D6 and pick up D♭6 to ring in M.39 on beat 2. (There is plenty of time for this switch.)

The tower swing notes represent the "morning bells" in the original song lyrics. There will likely be questions about which notes are supposed to be tower swung. Here's how it works:

- M.1-2, 3-4: E♭4, B♭4 and E♭5 are tied notes. Do a double tower swing without ringing again. Follow the arrows to swing on the correct beats. G5, C6 and G6 are the only notes that should be rung in M.2 and M.4.
- M.5, 9, 13: Let melody notes be heard each time they enter. Do not tower swing melody notes.
- M.25-28: The tower swings apply only to the whole notes. E♭6 and B♭6 ring normally.

Page 55 – A Folk Tune
Beat 1 of each measure should be slightly accented for a "lilting" feel.

Page 56 – O Come, Little Children
This piece is suitable for the Christmas season. Watch for dynamic changes between legato and staccato notes. The rung melody should always be heard.

Page 61 – Ring a Scale with Chords
Once the group has learned this piece, ask them to stand beside different people so the bells are out of order. This will emphasize counting instead of simply waiting for one's turn in the scale line.

FREQUENTLY ASKED QUESTIONS

Q: Why can't I circle my notes?

A: *All notes relate to each other in a piece; circles isolate notes. Instead of circling or labeling each note, beginners may highlight the entire line/space on which their notes are found. Later, only highlight notes that need special attention, or draw an arrow pointing to them.*

Q: What if I miss my note, or the clapper doesn't strike?

A: *The temptation is to quickly ring the bell, even though the beat has already passed. With handbells, the reverse of an old adage applies—better never than late! Ringing late makes it more obvious that you made a mistake. It can also throw everyone else off the beat. Instead, let it go and come back in on your next note. Above all, keep counting!*

Q: Page turns! I can't put my bell down, turn the page, pick up my bell again, and ring in time.

A: *Have two people share a music stand. Plan ahead for which ringer has the most time to turn the page. Another trick is to memorize the notes just before or after the turn.*

TIP: Turning pages while wearing gloves is tricky! Fold up the corner of the page to make it easier to grab.

Q: How can I ring my usual notes plus accidentals and/or unassigned bells? I need three hands!

A: *Instead of damping a bell on your shoulder, damp it on the table to free one of your hands. Table damp notes at the end of their note value and pick up the other bell right away, whether you are changing to an accidental or returning to your primary bell. Plan a strategy and practice it. Also, a neighboring ringer may be free to ring an extra note at that point. Work out a plan together—it's all about teamwork!*

TIP: To mark your music, place a downward arrow beside the note of the bell to be table damped. Circle the note to be picked up—both the accidental and your next primary note.

Q: In the example below, F5 is written as both an eighth note and a dotted half note on beat one, and it reappears as another eighth note on the "and" of beat 2. How do I handle this?

A: *In this example, F5 is part of both the melody and the chord. Ring on beat 1 and ring again on the "and" of beat 2. Do not damp either time—let the second note finish out the value of the dotted half note.*